Rice

Edited by Rebecca Stefoff

Text © 1990 by Garrett Educational Corporation
First Published in the United States in 1990
by Garrett Educational Corporation,
130 E. 13th Street, Ada, OK 74820

First Published 1989 by A&C Black (Publishers) Limited, London
with the title RICE
1989 © A&C Black (Publishers) Ltd.

Library of Congress Cataloging-in-Publication Data

Thomson, Ruth.
    Rice / Ruth Thomson ; photographs by Prodeepta Das.
    p.   cm. - (Threads)
    Incudes index.
    Summary: Shows where rice comes from and how it is grown, cooked
and used.
    ISBN 0-944483-71-2
    1. Rice-Juvenile literature. 2. Cookery (Rice)-Juvenile literature. 3. Rice-
Utilization-Juvenile literature. [1. Rice. 2. Cookery-Rice.] I. Das, Prodeepta, ill.
II. Title. III. Series.
SB191.R5T49   1990
633.1'8-dc20
                                                        90-40367
                                                          CIP
                                                          AC

Rice

Ruth Thomson

Photographs by Prodeepta Das

Contents

GEC GARRETT EDUCATIONAL CORPORATION

Have you tasted any of these?

Rice and tuna salad

Rice pudding

Egg fried rice

Rice crispies with milk

Curried rice

Rice and beans

3

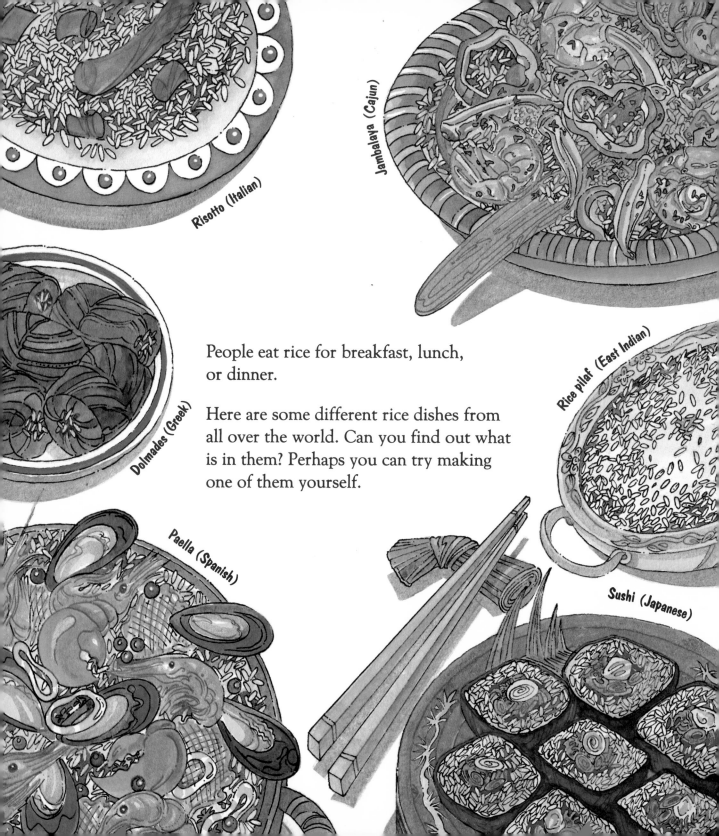

Risotto (Italian)

Jambalaya (Cajun)

Dolmades (Greek)

Rice pilaf (East Indian)

People eat rice for breakfast, lunch, or dinner.

Here are some different rice dishes from all over the world. Can you find out what is in them? Perhaps you can try making one of them yourself.

Paella (Spanish)

Sushi (Japanese)

Raw rice

Collect some different kinds of rice from the supermarket and take a close look at them. Rice comes in different colors and shapes.

Feel, smell, and taste some of the rice, It doesn't taste very nice, does it? It's hard and gritty. But once it's been cooked, it tastes quite different.

Long grain rice

Brown   White

Brown   White

Short grain rice

5

Cooked rice

Try boiling some rice

You will need

Saucepan with close-fitting lid

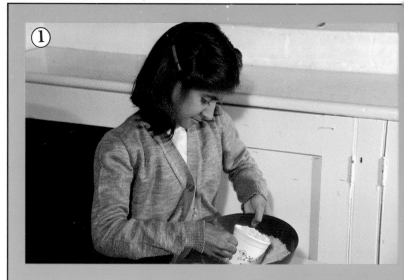

Long grain rice

Large strainer

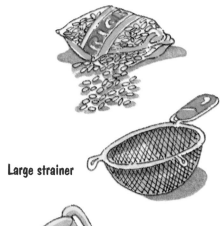

Tea cup

Water

A stove or hot plate
(Ask an adult to help you with this)

How to do it

1. Measure out one cup of rice. The rice should be level with the top of the cup.

2. Pour rice into the strainer and wash it under water until the water that runs through is no longer cloudy.

3. Put the rice into the saucepan and add exactly 1½ cups of water. Put the lid on the pan. Bring the water to a boil.

③

④

⑤

5. How many cups of rice have you got now? Measure out the rice and see. What do you think has happened?

Try cooking different types of rice and compare them.

Turn the heat down as low as possible and let the water simmer for about 20 minutes, until it has almost all been absorbed by the rice. The rice will look fluffy and there will be holes on the surface where bubbles of steam have escaped.

Turn off the heat, but leave the covered saucepan on the stove for another five minutes.

Long grain rice is fluffy, and the grains are separate.

Short grain rice is shiny, translucent and sticky.

Taste them with your eyes shut. Can you tell the difference?

7

What is rice?

The rice we eat comes from the seeds of rice plants. Here are some, shown close up. You can see the seeds at the ends of the stalks. This is only one kind of rice plant. There are more than seven thousand different kinds.

Can you think of any other plants that look like rice?

Rice is a type of grass, as are wheat, oats, barley, millet, corn, and rye. They are often called cereal crops.

Millet

Oats

Barle

Ric

Corn

Wheat

Rye

Each seed of the rice plant has a tough outer husk. Inside is a grain of rice. Around the grain, there's a protective skin, called bran.

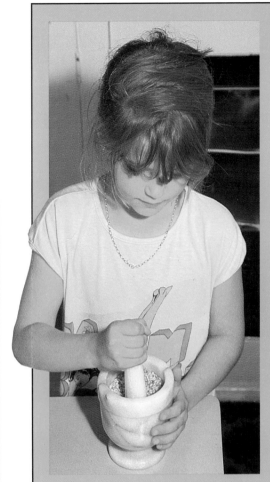

The rice we buy in stores has been milled to get rid of the tough outer skins. Sometimes this is done by pounding the rice seeds with a long pole. Milling by hand is very hard work, so it's often done by machine. The rice is put into metal drums, and rollers turning inside the drums remove the husks from the rice.

Brown rice still has some of the bran left on it. See if you can turn brown rice into white rice by milling it in a mortar and pestle like the one in the photograph, or by rubbing it on a wire strainer. Most of the vitamins in rice are contained in the bran skin, so brown rice is better for you than white rice.

9

Grow your own rice

Each grain of rice contains the beginnings of a new rice plant and some food for the plant as it grows.

You can try growing your own rice plants. See if you can grow some different kinds.

You will need

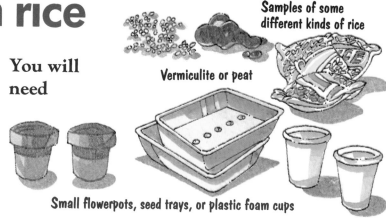

Samples of some different kinds of rice

Vermiculite or peat

Small flowerpots, seed trays, or plastic foam cups

How to do it

① ②

1. Fill the flowerpots with vermiculite or peat. Sprinkle the rice on the surface and water it. Make sure you keep the peat or vermiculite damp.

2. Put some of the pots in a warm place, such as a sunny windowsill or a radiator; put some in a cool place, or outside. After a few days, some of the rice will begin to sprout. Which rice grows best? What happens to the grains of rice that don't sprout? Do white rice and brown rice grow equally well?

Rice farming

Keep a record of your rice as it grows. How tall does it get? Young rice plants like these are usually grown in a nursery, or in the corner of a field.

When the rice plants get a bit taller and stronger, they are transplanted into flooded fields called rice paddies.

Before the rice is planted, the paddies are flooded with just the right amount of water. Can you see the ditches going across the fields? These bring water from the river. The little walls around the fields hold the water.

The fields are plowed to turn over the soil and soften the mud. The oxen pull the plow, but how else do you think their work helps?

The young rice is usually transplanted in rows, with plenty of space between them, which makes it easier to weed the fields later on. Do you think this job looks easy?

The rice paddies in these pictures are in India, but rice is grown in many other parts of Asia, as well as North and South America, the Soviet Union, Europe, and Africa.

As it ripens, the rice turns golden brown. When the crop is ready to harvest, the farmer drains the paddy and lets the mud harden. Most rice is still cut by hand, usually with a curved knife called a sickle. The rice is bundled together into sheaves, which are left to dry for a few days before being collected.

The cut rice has to be threshed to separate the grains from the stalks. In some places, the rice sheaves are beaten by hand against a log, or are trampled by animals. Some farmers have threshing machines, which make the job much quicker.

13

To get rid of dirt and pieces of stalk, the grains are put in a strainer or a flat bamboo basket and shaken back and forth. This is called winnowing. Can you see how the stalks, or chaff, and dirt collect at the top of the basket? These blow away in the wind or are dumped out. The heavier rice stays in the basket.

You can try winnowing by mixing rice with some grass or straw and shaking it in a large, flat tray or basket. It's best to do this outside on a windy day, if possible.

14

The clean rice is dried so that it will not decay. Then it is stored in pots or bags in barns until it is needed for milling.

On some of the bigger rice farms, machines are used to plow the land and plant the rice seed. Enormous combine harvesters reap the crops and the rice is taken to modern rice mills, which can produce up to 1,000 tons of milled rice each day.

Machines like these combine harvesters are too expensive for many farmers. They are also too large to be used on small paddies.

Rice for special occasions

Rice is such an important food for most of the people in the world that it is often used in celebrations. Sweet rice, or pilaf, is often served at Muslim celebrations. You can find a recipe for it at the end of this book.

At weddings, people sometimes throw rice over the bride for good luck. Have you ever been to a wedding where this was done?

The custom of throwing rice at weddings originated in India. At Hindu weddings, the bridegroom throws three handfuls of rice over the bride and she does the same to him. In the wedding picture on the left, you can see the rice in a bowl at the front of the picture.

In India, on religious holidays, people decorate their doorsteps with Rangoli patterns to welcome visitors. The patterns are made with rice flour colored with vegetable dyes.

You can make your own Rangoli patterns, using rice powder mixed with powder paints.

17

Eating rice

How many ways can you eat rice? In India it is the custom to roll rice into little balls by hand.

In Japan and other Far Eastern countries, people use chopsticks.

ave you ever tried using chopsticks?

s not difficult, once you've learned the knack.
his is one way of using them.

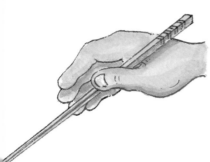 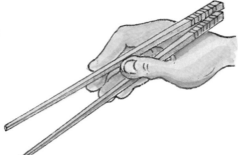 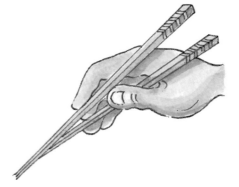

Rest one chopstick on ur fourth finger and ld it there with your umb.

2. Hold the other chopstick between the tip of your thumb and your forefinger.

3. Pick up food by moving the top chopstick toward the bottom one, like a tweezer.

you put the bowl uite close to your outh, you're less kely to drop ieces of food.

Make your own rice dishes

Rice does not have much flavor of its own.
Put a little cooked rice into lots of separate
bowls and add a different flavor to each one.
Which do you prefer?

Tomato ketchup

Soy sauce

Salad dressing

Sugar

Yogurt

Salt

You can use cooked rice to make lots of simple dishes. Mix it with some of these things to make a delicious salad.

Try making rice and carrot loaf

You will need

Pepper to taste

2 tablespoons oil

1 cup cooked rice

Margarine (for greasing pan)

1 egg

1 cup grated cheddar cheese

1 tsp. salt

1 tsp. parsley

3 cups grated carrots (about 250g)

Equipment

Egg whisk

Wooden spoon

Saucepan

Small mixing bowl

Grater

Oiled paper

Oven, set to 180° C (375° F) Gas Mark 5

Large mixing bowl

Loaf pan

How to do it

1.   Be sure to get permission before you start. Boil the rice until it is soft (see the recipe on page 6). Peel the carrots and grate them on the fine side of a grater. Put them in a big bowl. Beat the egg with a whisk in a small bowl.

2.   Grate the cheese on the fine side of the grater.

Bake in the oven for about 30 minutes, until the mixture looks set.

Leave the pan to cool and then turn the loaf out on a plate. Serve hot or cold in slices.

3. Mix the cooked rice into the carrots. Add the cheese, salt, pepper, parsley, and egg.

4. Grease a loaf pan and spoon in the mixture. Press it down with the back of the spoon to make it smooth.

Rice is a staple food

Did you know that these are made from rice?

Edible rice paper

Pancakes

Rice noodles

Rice flour for making cakes

More than half the people in the world eat rice as their staple food. That means they eat rice almost every day. In South America people eat corn as their staple food, and in Africa people eat sorghum, millet, and cassava.

What is your staple food? It might be potatoes. It might be pasta or bread; both of these are made from wheat. Perhaps it's rice? If so, you are one of seven hundred million people who eat rice almost every day!

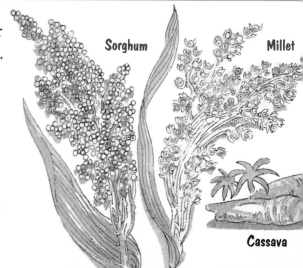

Sorghum

Millet

Cassava

More thing to do

1. China grows a third of all the rice that is grown in the world. Find out which other countries are major producers. Many countries grow only enough rice for themselves and don't sell it to other countries. Look on packages of rice in stores and supermarkets to see where the rice was grown.

2. Rice contains starch, which is food for the new rice plant as it grows and is also food for us. Find out what other kinds of food have starch in them. Many people in the world can't afford much else to eat besides rice. Do you think this is enough? Find out what other kinds of foods are important to eat besides starchy foods.

3. Rice starch is used to make edible rice paper and wine. It is also used as a stiffener for clothes and to make glue. Try dipping a handkerchief in a mixture of starch and water. Then hang it up to dry. What does it feel like when it's dry?

4. Other products, such as baskets and hats, are made from the rice plant. See what you can find out about them.

5. Rice is a seed. Try growing some other edible seeds, such as beans, peas, or lentils.

6. Try cooking sweet rice. Be sure to get permission before you begin. You will need: knife, mixing bowl, saucepan, stove or hot plate, paper towels, 2 onions, 2 cups uncooked rice, a handful of raisins, a handful of sliced almonds, ⅛ lb. butter, 3½ cups hot water, a pinch of tumeric, 6 tsp. of sugar; also 4 whole black cardamoms, 4 small green cardamoms, 4 cloves, and one small stick of cinnamon crushed together.

Put the rice in a mixing bowl and cover with water. Leave for 15 minutes and then drain. Slice the onions and fry them in butter until they are golden brown. Put half the onions aside on the paper towel. To the remaining onions, add the raisins, almonds, a pinch of tumeric, the crushed spices, and the rice. Fry on a low heat for 5 minutes. Add the water slowly and then the sugar. Simmer for 10 minutes or until the rice is cooked. Serve warm, with the rest of the onions on top. (This is a simple recipe for sweet rice. The rice shown in the photograph on page 16 also includes saffron, which gives a yellow color.)

Index